Disney SONGS
FOR OCARINA

*Based on the "Winnie the Pooh" works, by A.A. Milne and E.H. Shepard

© Disney

The following songs are the property of:

Bourne Co.
Music Publishers
5 West 37th Street
New York, NY 10018

WHEN YOU WISH UPON A STAR
WHISTLE WHILE YOU WORK
WHO'S AFRAID OF THE BIG BAD WOLF?

ISBN 978-1-5400-2674-3

HAL•LEONARD®

Visit Hal Leonard Online at
www.halleonard.com

Contact Us:
Hal Leonard
7777 West Bluemound Road
Milwaukee, WI 53213
Email: info@halleonard.com

In Europe contact:
Hal Leonard Europe Limited
Distribution Centre, Newmarket Road
Bury St Edmunds, Suffolk, IP33 3YB
Email: info@halleonardeurope.com

In Australia contact:
Hal Leonard Australia Pty. Ltd.
4 Lentara Court
Cheltenham, Victoria, 3192 Australia
Email: info@halleonard.com.au

BE OUR GUEST
from BEAUTY AND THE BEAST

Music by ALAN MENKEN
Lyrics by HOWARD ASHMAN

Be our guest! Be our guest! Put our ser-vice to the test. Tie your nap-kin 'round your neck, *che-rie,* and we pro-vide the rest. *Soup du jour!* Hot *hors d'oeuvres!* Why, we on-ly live to serve. Try the grey stuff, it's de-li-cious! Don't be-lieve me? Ask the dish-es! They can sing! They can dance! Af-ter all Miss, this is France! And a din-ner here is nev-er sec-ond best. Go on, un-fold your men-u, take a glance, and then you'll be our guest, *oui,* our guest! Be our guest!

BIBBIDI-BOBBIDI-BOO
(The Magic Song)
from CINDERELLA

Words by JERRY LIVINGSTON
Music by MACK DAVID and AL HOFFMAN

Brightly

Sa - la - ga - doo - la men - chic - ka boo - la bib - bi - di - bob - bi - di - boo,

put 'em to - geth - er and what have you got? Bib - bi - di - bob - bi - di - boo, Sa - la - ga - do - la men - chic - ka boo - la

bib - bi - di - bob - bi - di - boo, it - 'll do mag - ic be - lieve it or not, bib - bi - di - bob - bi - di - boo.

Sa - la - ga - doo - la means men - chic - ka boo - le - roo, but the thing - a - ma - bob that does the job is

bib - bi - di - bob - bi - di - boo. Sa - la - ga - doo - la men - chic - ka boo - la bib - bi - di - bob - bi - di - boo,

put 'em to - geth - er and what have you got? Bib - bi - di - bob - bi - di, bib - bi - di - bob - bi - di, bib - bi - di - bob - bi - di - boo.

CAN YOU FEEL THE LOVE TONIGHT

from THE LION KING

Music by ELTON JOHN
Lyrics by TIM RICE

Pop Ballad

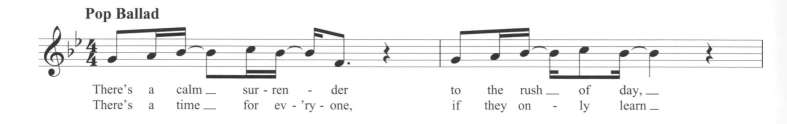

There's a calm sur - ren - der   to the rush of day,
There's a time for ev - 'ry - one,   if they on - ly learn

when the land of the roll - ing world   can be turned a - way.
that the twist - ing ka - lei - do - scope   moves us all in turn.

An en - chant - ed mo - ment,   and it sees me through.
There's a rhyme and rea - son   to the wild out - doors

It's e - nough for this rest - less war - rior   just to be with you.
when the heart of this star - crossed voy - ag - er   beats in time with yours.   And

can you feel the love to - night?   It is where we are.

It's e - nough _____ for this wide - eyed ___ wan-der- er

that we got this far. _____ And can you feel ___ the love ___

_____ to - night, _____ how it's laid ___ to rest? ____

It's e - nough _____ to make kings ___ and ____ vag - a - bonds ___ be -

1.

lieve the ver - y best. ____

2.

It's e - nough _____ to make

kings ___ and ___ vag - a - bonds ___ be - lieve the ver - y best. _____

CHIM CHIM CHER-EE

from MARY POPPINS

Words and Music by RICHARD M. SHERMAN
and ROBERT B. SHERMAN

Lightly, with gusto

DO YOU WANT TO BUILD A SNOWMAN?

from FROZEN

Music and Lyrics by KRISTEN ANDERSON-LOPEZ
and ROBERT LOPEZ

COLORS OF THE WIND
from POCAHONTAS

Music by ALAN MENKEN
Lyrics by STEPHEN SCHWARTZ

Deliberately

You think you own what-ev-er land you land on, the earth is just a dead thing you can

claim; but I know ev-'ry rock and tree and crea-ture has a

life, has a spir - it, has a name. You think the on - ly peo - ple who are

peo - ple are the peo - ple who look and think like you, but

if you walk the foot-steps of a stran - ger, you'll learn things you nev - er knew you nev - er

knew. _____ Have you ev - er heard the wolf cry to the blue corn moon, or

9

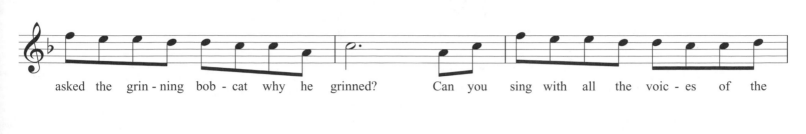

asked the grin - ning bob - cat why he grinned? Can you sing with all the voic - es of the

moun - tain? Can you paint with all the col - ors of the wind? _____ Can you

paint with all the col - ors of the wind? How high does the

syc - a-more grow? If you cut it down, _ then you'll nev - er know. _____ And you'll

nev - er hear the wolf cry to the blue corn moon, for wheth - er we are white or cop - per -

skinned, we need to sing with all the voic - es of the moun - tain, need to

paint with all the col - ors of the wind. You can own the earth and still all you'll

own is earth un - til you can paint with all the col - ors of the wind. _____

EVERMORE
from BEAUTY AND THE BEAST

Music by ALAN MENKEN
Lyrics by TIM RICE

Sturdy Ballad

I was the one who had it all; I was the mas-ter of my

fate. I nev-er need-ed an-y-bod-y in my life;

I learned the truth too late. I'll nev-er shake a-way the
I rage a-gainst the trials of

pain. I close my eyes, but she's still there.
love. I curse the fad-ing of the light.

I let her steal in-to my mel-an-chol-y heart; it's more than I can
Though she's al-read-y flown so far be-yond my reach, she's nev-er out of

bear. Now I know she'll nev-er leave me, e-ven
sight. Now I know she'll nev-er leave me, e-ven

FOR THE FIRST TIME IN FOREVER

from FROZEN

Music and Lyrics by KRISTEN ANDERSON-LOPEZ
and ROBERT LOPEZ

With excitement

The win-dow is o - pen! So's ___ that door! ___ I

did-n't know they did that an - y - more. ___ Who knew we owned ___ eight thou - sand sal - ad

plates? For years I've roamed ___ these emp - ty halls. ___

Why have a ball - room with ___ no balls? ___ Fi - nal - ly, ___ they're o - p'ning up ___ the

gates! There'll be ac - tu - al real ___ live peo - ple;

it-'ll be to-tal-ly strange. ___ But, wow! Am I ___ so read-y for ___ this

Expressively

change! 'Cause for the first time in for-ev-er, there'll be

mu-sic, there'll __ be light. ___ For the first time in for-ev-

- er, I'll be danc-ing through the night. ___ Don't

know if I'm e-lat-ed or gas-sy, but I'm some-where in ___ that

zone. 'Cause for the first time in for-ev-er, _____

I won't be _____ a-lone. ___

HAKUNA MATATA

from THE LION KING

Music by ELTON JOHN
Lyrics by TIM RICE

HE'S A PIRATE

from PIRATES OF THE CARIBBEAN: THE CURSE OF THE BLACK PEARL

Music by KLAUS BADELT,
GEOFFREY ZANELLI and HANS ZIMMER

HOW DOES A MOMENT LAST FOREVER

from BEAUTY AND THE BEAST

Music by ALAN MENKEN
Lyrics by TIM RICE

HOW FAR I'LL GO
from MOANA

Music and Lyrics by
LIN-MANUEL MIRANDA

Moderately, in 2

I JUST CAN'T WAIT TO BE KING
from *THE LION KING*

Music by ELTON JOHN
Lyrics by TIM RICE

IN SUMMER

from FROZEN

Music and Lyrics by KRISTEN ANDERSON-LOPEZ
and ROBERT LOPEZ

Moderately, in 2

(small note optional)

Bees - 'll buzz, kids - 'll blow dan - de - li - on fuzz, and I'll be do - ing what - ev - er snow does in sum - mer. A drink in my hand, my snow up a - gainst the burn - ing sand, prob - 'ly get - ting gor - geous - ly tanned in sum - mer. I'll fi - n'lly see a sum - mer breeze blow a - way a win - ter storm, and find out what hap - pens to sol - id wa - ter when it gets warm. And I can't wait to see what my bud - dies all think of me. Just i - mag - ine how much cool - er I'll be in sum - mer!

KISS THE GIRL

from THE LITTLE MERMAID

Music by ALAN MENKEN
Lyrics by HOWARD ASHMAN

Moderately

There you see her sitting there a-cross the way. She don't got a lot to say, but there's some-thing a-bout her. And you don't know why, but you're dy-ing to try. You wan-na kiss the girl.

Yes, you want her. Look at her, you know you do. Pos-si-ble she wants you, too. There is one way to ask her. It don't take a word, not a sin-gle word, go on and kiss the girl.

Sha la la la la la, my oh my. Look like the boy too shy. Ain't gon-na kiss the girl.

Sha la la la la la, ain't that sad. Ain't it a shame, too bad. He gon-na miss the girl.

You've got-ta kiss the girl. Go on and kiss the girl.

LAVA
from LAVA

Music and Lyrics by
JAMES FORD MURPHY

Easy half-time feel

MICKEY MOUSE MARCH

from THE MICKEY MOUSE CLUB

Words and Music by
JIMMIE DODD

Brightly

Mick - ey Mouse Club! Mick - ey Mouse Club!

Who's the lead - er of the club that's made for you and me?
Hey, there! Hi, there! Ho, there! You're as wel - come as can be!

1.
M - I - C - K - E - Y M - O - U - S - E!

2.
E! Mick - ey Mouse! _____ Mick - ey Mouse! _____ For -

ev - er let us hold our ban - ner high! (High! High! High!)

Come a - long and sing a song and join the jam - bo - ree!

M - I - C - K - E - Y M - O - U - S - E!

SEIZE THE DAY

from NEWSIES

Music by ALAN MENKEN
Lyrics by JACK FELDMAN

Hymn-like

O - pen the gates and seize the day. Don't be a-fraid and don't de - lay.

Noth - ing can break us. No one can make us give our rights a - way. A -

rise and seize the day. Now is the time to seize the day.

(Now is the time to seize the day.) Send out the call and join the fray. (Send out the call and join the fray.)

Wrongs will __ be right - ed if we're __ u - nit - ed. Let us __ seize __ the

day. _____ Neigh - bor to neigh - bor, _____ fa - ther to

son, _____ one for all and all __ for one.

SUPERCALIFRAGILISTICEXPIALIDOCIOUS

from MARY POPPINS

Words and Music by RICHARD M. SHERMAN
and ROBERT B. SHERMAN

Brightly

Su - per - cal - i - frag - il - is - tic - ex - pi - al - i - do - cious!

E - ven though the sound of it is some - thing quite a - tro - cious,

if you say it loud e - nough, you'll al - ways sound pre - co - cious.

Su - per - cal - i - frag - il - is - tic - ex - pi - al - i - do - cious!

Um did - dle did - dle did - dle, um did - dle ay! Um did - dle did - dle did - dle, um did - dle ay! Be -

THAT'S HOW YOU KNOW

from ENCHANTED

Music by ALAN MENKEN
Lyrics by STEPHEN SCHWARTZ

Freely

How does she know _____ you love her? ___ How does she

know _____ she's yours? How does she know

that you love her? How do you show her you love her? How does she know

that you real - ly, real - ly, tru - ly love her? It's not e-nough to take __

__ the one you love for grant - ed. _____ You must re - mind her, or __

_____ she'll be in-clined to say: "How do I know _____

_____ he loves me? _____ How do I know _____

_____ he's mine?" Well, does he leave a lit-tle note to

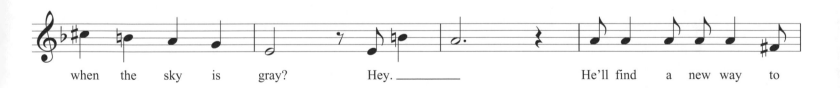

tell you you are on his mind? _____ Send you yel-low flow - ers

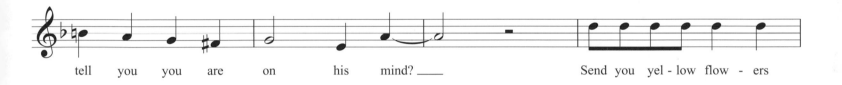

when the sky is gray? Hey. _____ He'll find a new way to

show you _____ a lit - tle bit ev - 'ry day. _____ That's how _____ you

know, that's how _____ you know he's _____ your love.

WHEN YOU WISH UPON A STAR

from PINOCCHIO

Words by NED WASHINGTON
Music by LEIGH HARLINE

WHISTLE WHILE YOU WORK

from SNOW WHITE AND THE SEVEN DWARFS

Words by LARRY MOREY
Music by FRANK CHURCHILL

WHO'S AFRAID OF THE BIG BAD WOLF?

from THREE LITTLE PIGS

Words and Music by
FRANK CHURCHILL
Additional Lyric by ANN RONELL

A WHOLE NEW WORLD

from ALADDIN

Music by ALAN MENKEN
Lyrics by TIM RICE

WINNIE THE POOH*
from THE MANY ADVENTURES OF WINNIE THE POOH

Words and Music by RICHARD M. SHERMAN
and ROBERT B. SHERMAN

Tenderly

Deep in the hun - dred a - cre wood where Chris - to - pher

Rob - in plays, _____ you'll find the en - chant - ed neigh - bor -

hood of Chris - to - pher's child - hood days. _____ A

don - key named Ee - yore is his friend, and Kan - ga and lit - tle Roo; there's

Rab - bit, there's Pig - let and there's Owl, but most of all Win - nie the Pooh!

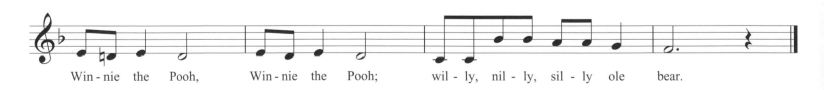

Win - nie the Pooh, Win - nie the Pooh, Win - nie the Pooh; stuffed with fluff, He's

Win - nie the Pooh, Win - nie the Pooh; wil - ly, nil - ly, sil - ly ole bear.

YO HO
(A Pirate's Life for Me)
from Disney Parks' Pirates of the Caribbean attraction

Words by XAVIER ATENCIO
Music by GEORGE BRUNS

In a robust manner

Yo ho, yo ho, a pi - rate's life for me. We

pil - lage, plun - der, we ri - fle and loot. Drink up me 'eart - ies, yo ho. We

kid - nap and rav - age and don't give a hoot. Drink up me 'eart - ies, yo ho. We're

ras - cals and scoun - drels, we're vil - lains and knaves. Drink up me 'eart - ies, yo ho. We're

dev - ils and black sheep, we're real - ly bad eggs. Drink up me 'eart - ies, yo ho.

Yo ho, yo ho, a pi - rate's life for me.

YOU CAN FLY! YOU CAN FLY! YOU CAN FLY!

from PETER PAN

Words by SAMMY CAHN
Music by SAMMY FAIN

YOU'RE WELCOME

from MOANA

Music and Lyrics by
LIN-MANUEL MIRANDA

YOU'VE GOT A FRIEND IN ME
from TOY STORY

Music and Lyrics by
RANDY NEWMAN

ZIP-A-DEE-DOO-DAH

from SONG OF THE SOUTH

Words by RAY GILBERT
Music by ALLIE WRUBEL

12-Hole Ocarina Fingering Chart